Name _____ Date _____

CLASSIFICATION

WHAT IS CLASSIFICATION?

Classification is a system of grouping things which are alike in some way. There is no perfect way to classify all things in the world. A classification system should have a useful purpose for the persons who are using it. One important purpose is to help you learn how things can be related.

Classify the objects below into four categories:

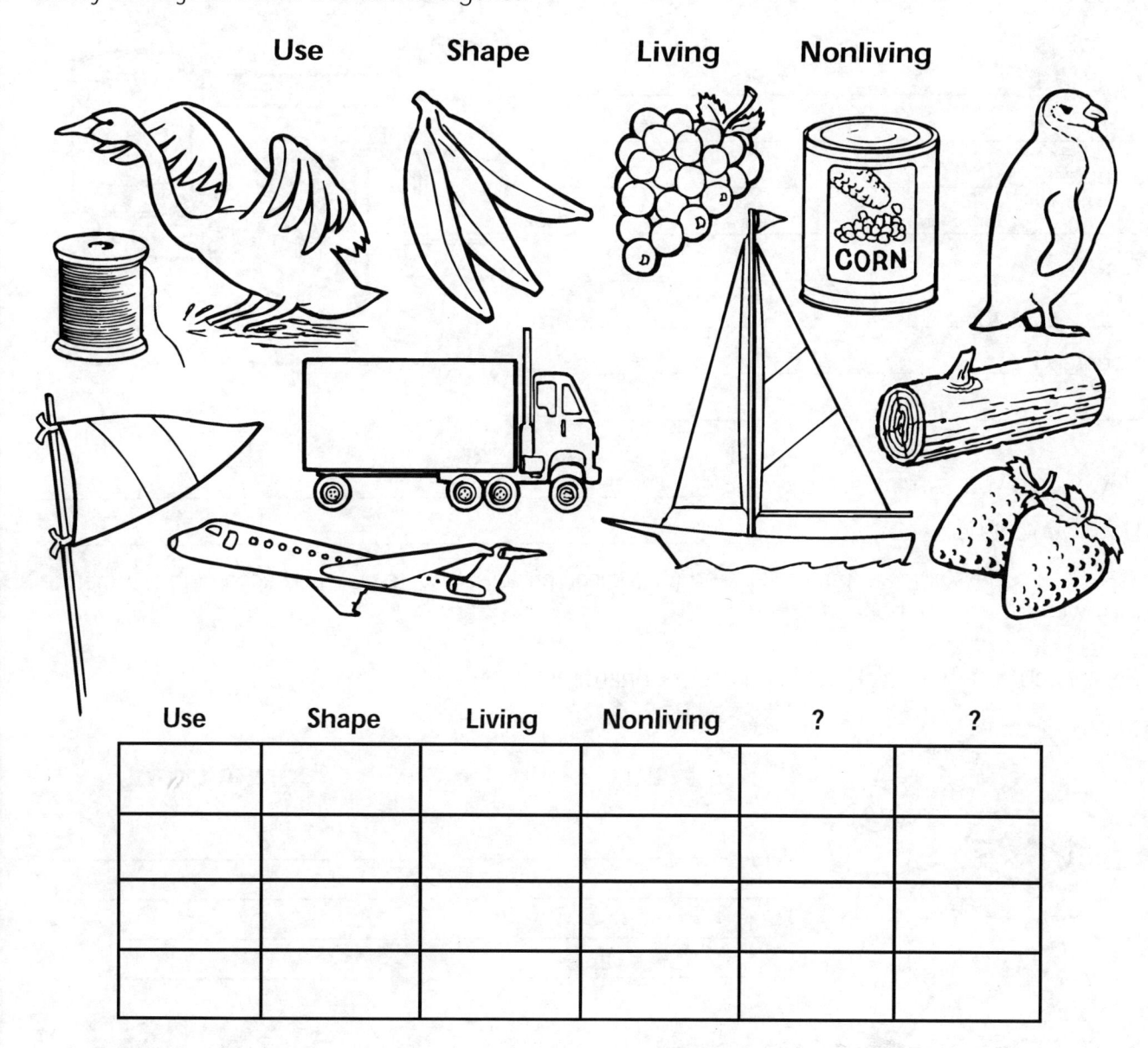

Use **Shape** **Living** **Nonliving**

Use	Shape	Living	Nonliving	?	?

Choose two other categories and fill them with appropriate objects. Can an object be in more than one category? Put a star by those which are.

DISCUSS

Is there only one correct way to put objects into categories?

MP3423 Classification   Copyright © 2000 – Milliken Publishing Co. All rights reserved.

Name _____   Date _____

CLASSIFICATION

WHY DO WE CLASSIFY?

We classify physical nonliving things as well as living things in order to organize them. If there were no method of classification in a library, you would never find the book you wanted. When you shop at a supermarket, you know where to find apples or milk because the products are organized.

If you owned a small hardware store, how would you display your products?

Counter 1 _____

Counter 2 _____

Counter 3 _____

Counter 4 _____

How would your system help shoppers? _____

How would it help you? _____

In very early days animals and other living (biological) organisms were classified according to whether they were harmful or nonharmful.

List animals you think might be harmful or nonharmful to humans.

HARMFUL	NONHARMFUL
_____	_____
_____	_____
_____	_____
_____	_____

DISCUSS

Do you think this early system of classification had a useful purpose? Why?

Name _____   Date _____

CLASSIFICATION

HISTORY OF CLASSIFICATION

A very simple early classification system was used by the Greek scholar, Aristotle. He grouped animals into two-legged and four-legged classes. Later, other scholars and scientists studied animals and plants. They recorded more detailed facts. But it was not until the 1700s that our modern system of classification was created by a Swedish botanist and doctor, Carolus Linnaeus. His aim was to name and describe all plants and animals in the world. Although the **Linnaean System** is still used by scientists all over the world, it has been expanded to include new and different living things as they are discovered. It will continue to grow as human knowledge grows.

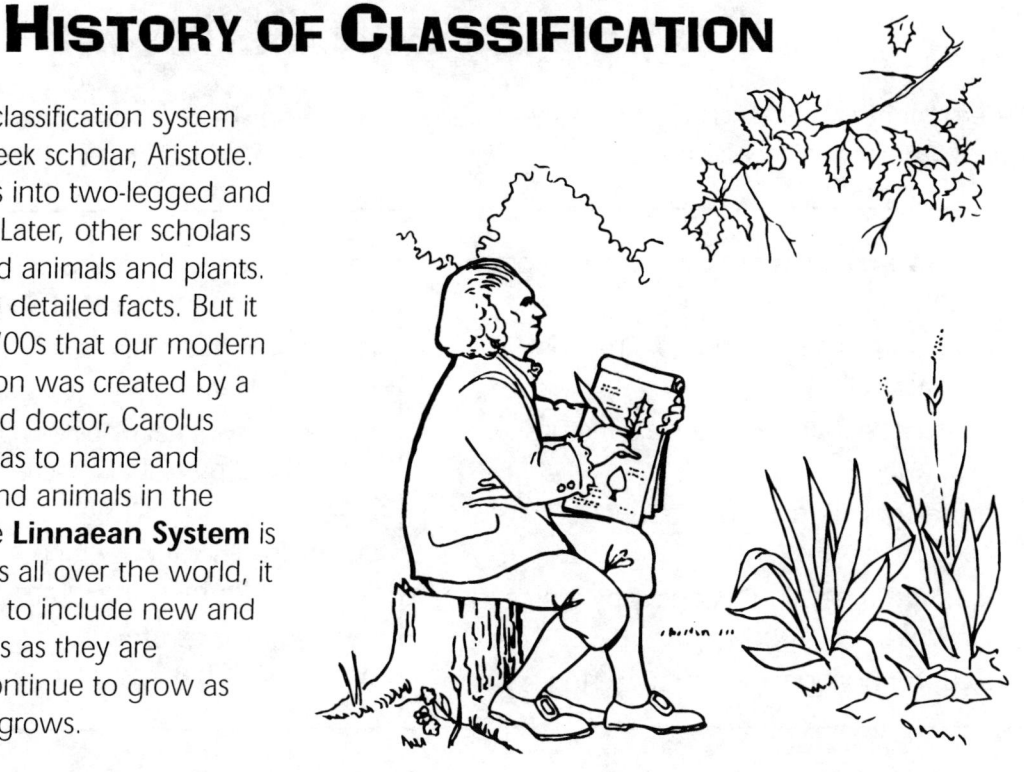

Research and write a short biography of Linnaeus.

ACTIVITY

Linnaeus copied his careful studies of each plant into a notebook. Bring three leaves from different trees or plants. Carefully study the shapes, stems, veins, colors and texture. Describe each leaf on a separate sheet of paper as Linnaeus did. When the leaves are dry, you can make a skeleton by placing one between two sheets of paper and pressing the top. You will then be able to study the veins. Compare your three studies for similarities and differences.

ACTIVITY

Collect five leaves from different trees or plants. Sort them into such classes as: smooth, serrated, lobed, compound, needles, color, etc. List ways they are alike and different.

_____

_____

Name _____   Date _____

CLASSIFICATION

CLASSIFICATION GLOSSARY

Understanding these terms will help as you study classification. There is room to add more words to your vocabulary as you learn them.

appearance: the outward look of a person or thing

category: a class or division in a system of classification

characteristic: a special trait, feature or quality

endangered: a thing in danger of becoming extinct

evolve: to develop gradually by a process of growth or change

extinct: no longer in use or existence

fossil: hardened remains or traces of plant or animal life of an earlier geological period

habitat: where a plant or animal naturally grows or lives

organism: animal or plant having different organs and parts that function together to maintain life and activity

structure: the arrangement of interrelated parts that form an organism

vestige: a trace or mark of something that once existed but has disappeared

Add other words and their definitions as you learn them.

Name _____ Date _____

CLASSIFICATION

APPEARANCE AND EXTERNAL STRUCTURES

Two characteristics scientists look at when classifying objects:
- Appearance—for example, rough skin
- External Structure—for example, tall

Appearance: A scientist begins to classify by studying the **appearance** of an object. The appearance includes its size, shape, color, and texture (how it feels when touched). These are known as **characteristics**.

Name some characteristics of a baseball: _____

Name some characteristics of a goldfish: _____

External Structures: Scientists know that the appearance of a thing depends upon its parts. The fish has fins, gills, scales, and a tail. These parts are called structures of the fish. Scientists group things together that have similar characteristics and structures.

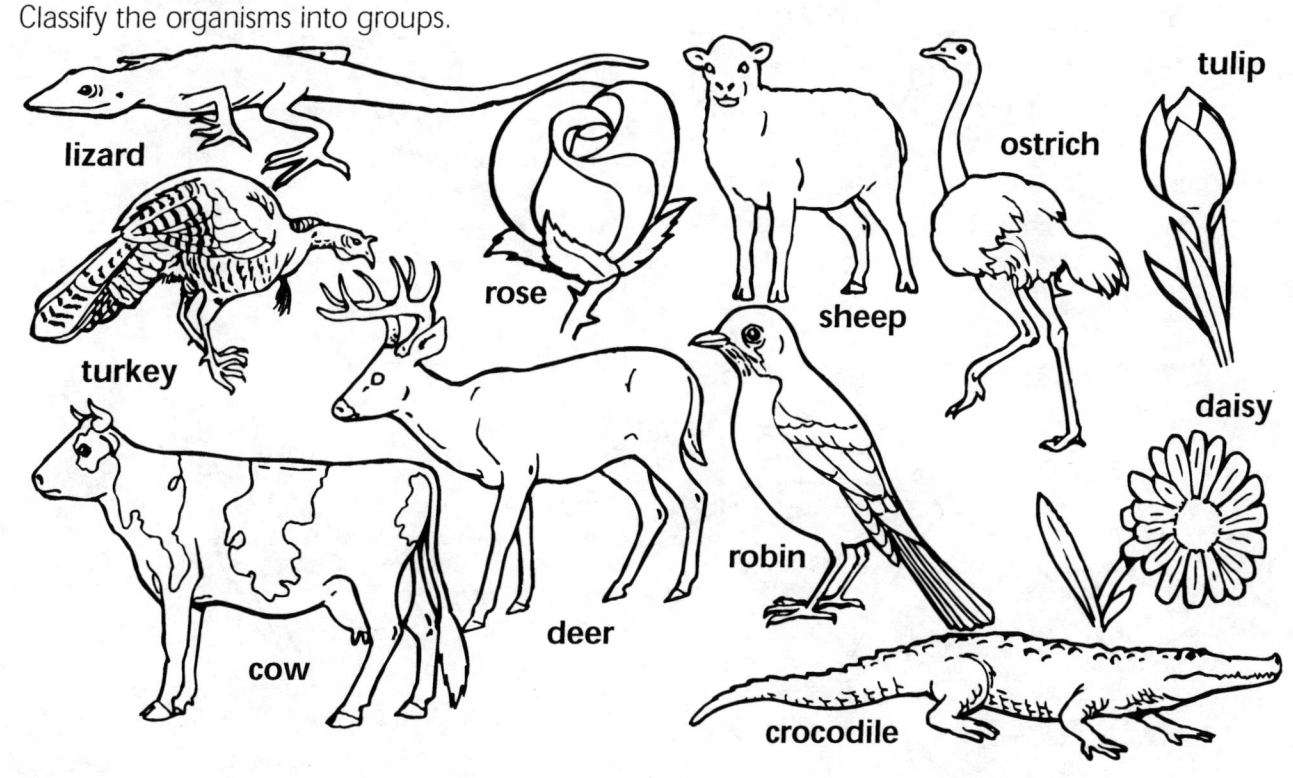

Classify the organisms into groups.

lizard, turkey, cow, rose, deer, sheep, robin, ostrich, crocodile, tulip, daisy

Group _____
Group _____
Group _____
Group _____
Group _____

Name _____ Date _____

CLASSIFICATION

INTERNAL STRUCTURE

Scientists learned that animals had likenesses which could not be seen by studying the appearance or outer structure of the living animals. So they began to look inside and study animal skeletons. They learned that a bat is more like a dog than a bird. A whale is more like a man than a fish, even though it lives in the ocean! It was found that different animals may not only have similar types of bones, but they may also have likenesses in the way their bones are joined. Bones are connected to other bones by joints. Joints in the skull are immovable, whereas joints in the arms and legs are movable.

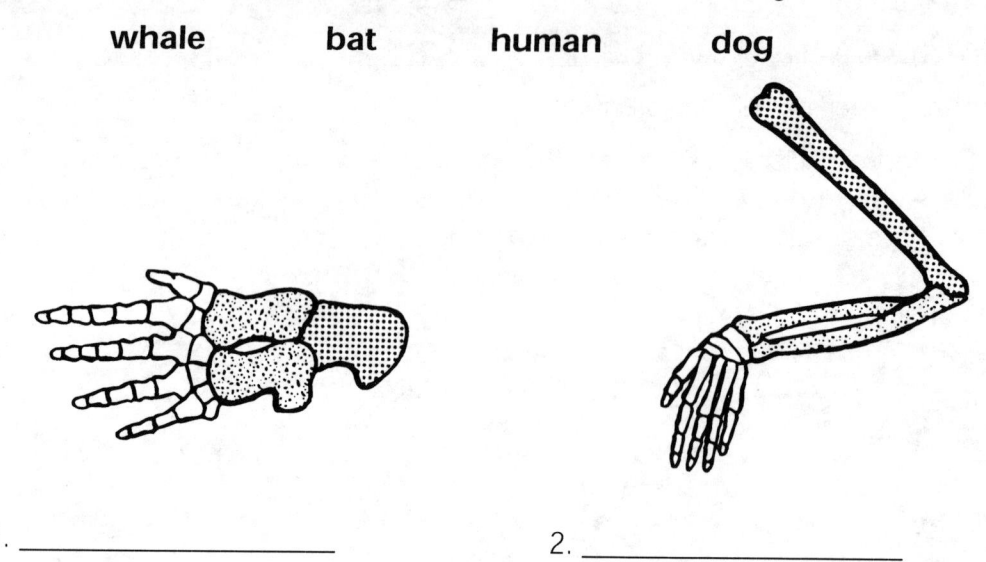

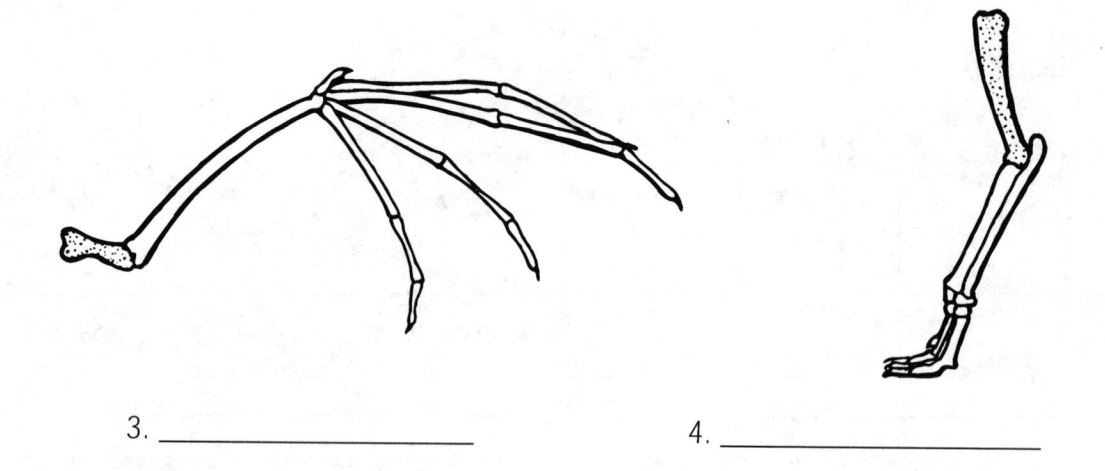

whale   bat   human   dog

1. _____

2. _____

3. _____

4. _____

5. Which skeleton is most like a person's? _____

6

Copyright © 2000 – Milliken Publishing Co. All rights reserved.

MP3423 Classification

CLASSIFYING LIVING THINGS

Biology is the science of living things. *Bio* is from the Greek language and means "life"; *ology* means "the scientific study of," so biology is the scientific study of living things. Each living thing must have most of the following characteristics:

1. move from place to place or make things inside it move around;
2. eat to get energy to breathe, move, and grow;
3. grow during its lifetime;
4. breathe in gases needed by its cells to grow, move, and use food;
5. change as it reacts to changes in the environment and body needs; and
6. reproduce its own kind to make the next generation.

All living things are biological forms of matter.

Draw an X in each section that describes the item named. Draw an O in each section that does not describe the item named.

	takes in food	grows	breathes	reacts	reproduces
tree	O	X	X	X	X
1. snake					
2. water					
3. horse					
4. salt					
5. mushroom					
6. soil					
7. grapevine					
8. air					
9. rock					

10. Biological forms of matter (living things) are: _____

CLASSIFICATION

REVIEW OF LIVING AND NONLIVING THINGS

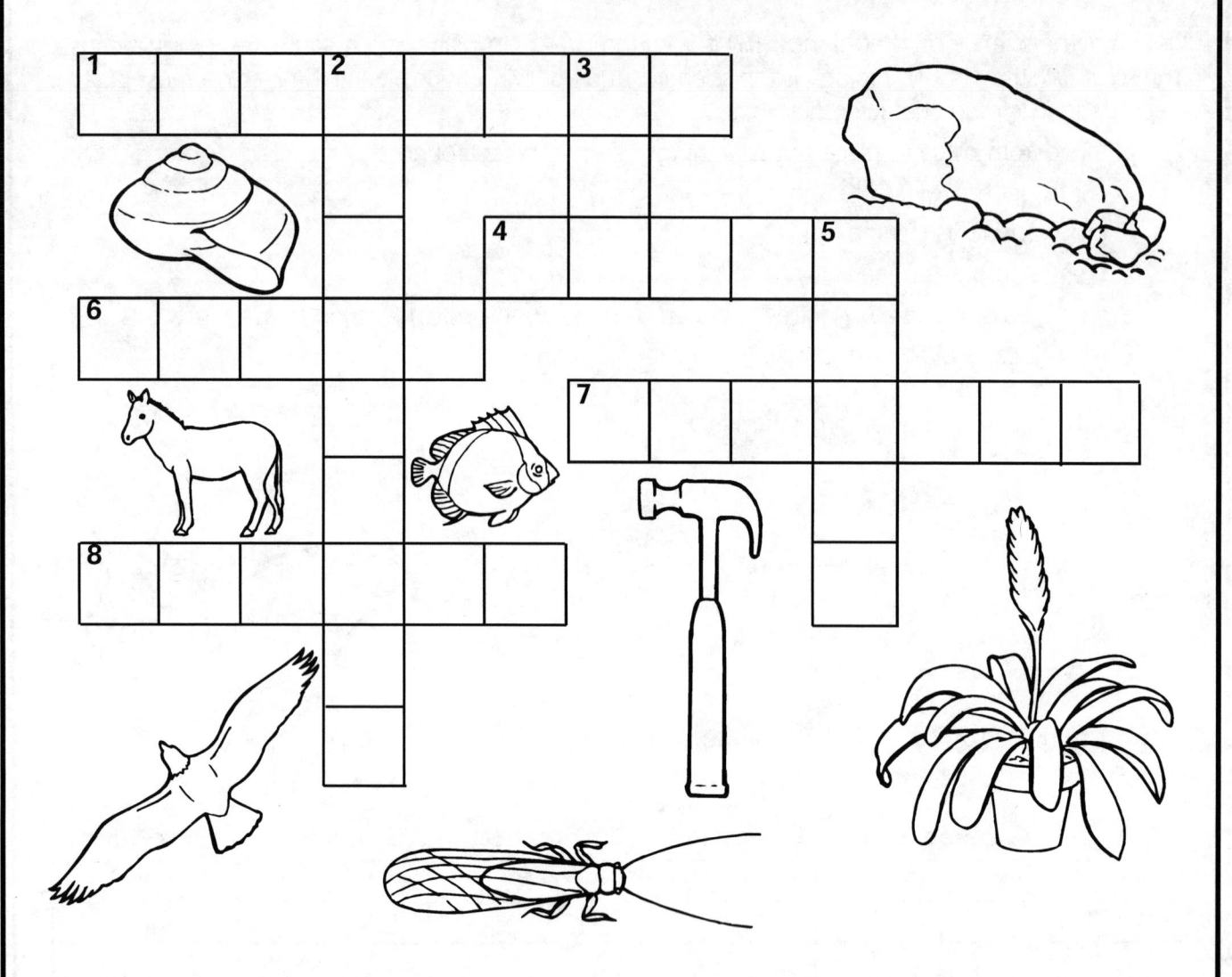

solid
grows
liquid
structure
biology
air
physical
group

ACROSS
1. Rocks are nonliving, _____ forms of matter.
4. A living thing _____ during its lifetime.
6. You _____ things when you classify them.
7. The science of living things
8. Matter that takes the shape of its container—it flows

DOWN
2. The arrangement of parts of an organism
3. A mixture of gases needed by plants and animals
5. Anything that has a definite shape or form.

Name _____   Date _____

CLASSIFICATION

ANIMAL KINGDOM—VERTEBRATES

Scientists divide biological organisms into five groups, known as the **Five Kingdoms**. The most familiar of these is the **Animal Kingdom**. All animals with a backbone or spine are called **vertebrates**.

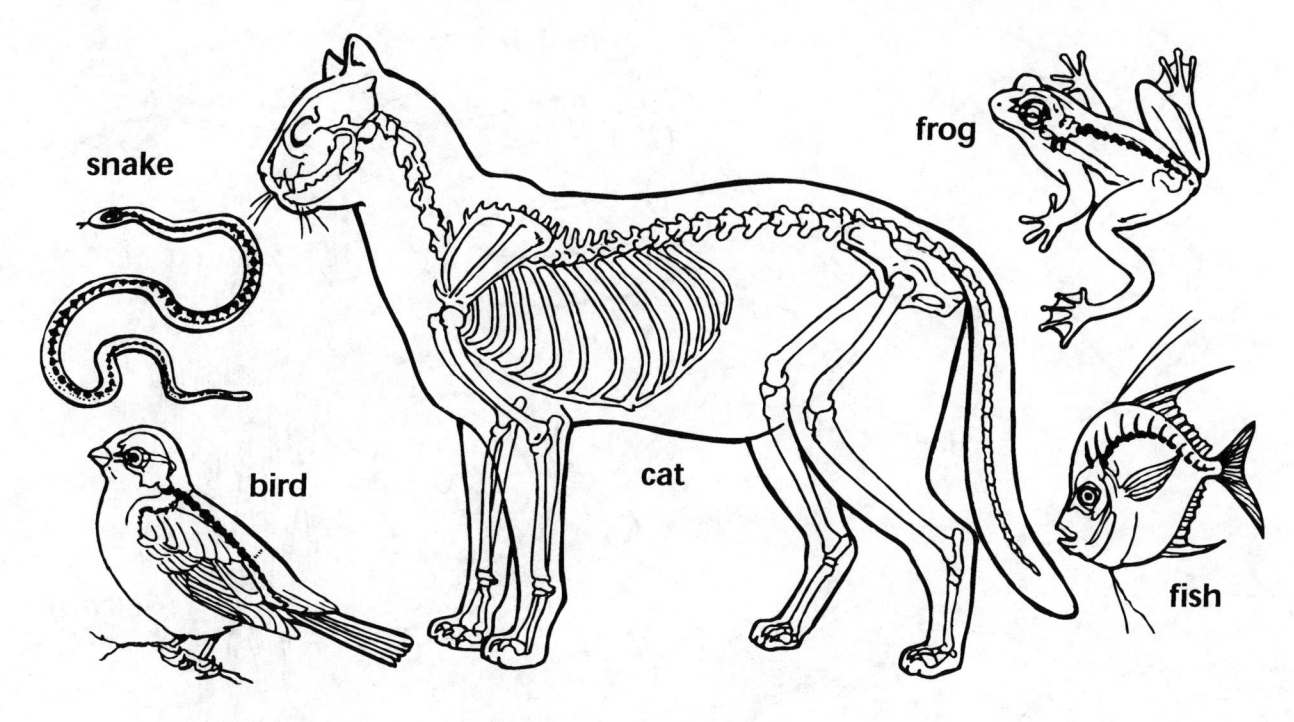

snake frog bird cat fish

What do you think the backbone does for an animal?

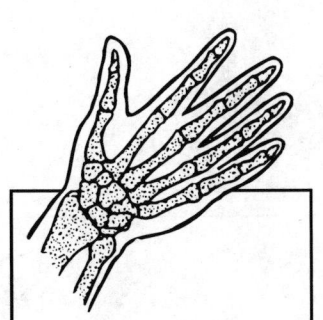

Would you have guessed that your hand has 27 bones in it? What do you think is the basic function of the hand? Try picking up an object without using your thumb.

Feel the bones in your hand. Draw a skeleton of it.

MP3423 Classification   9   Copyright © 2000 – Milliken Publishing Co. All rights reserved.

Name _____ Date _____

CLASSIFICATION

ANIMAL KINGDOM—INVERTEBRATES

Animals without a backbone or spine are **invertebrates**.

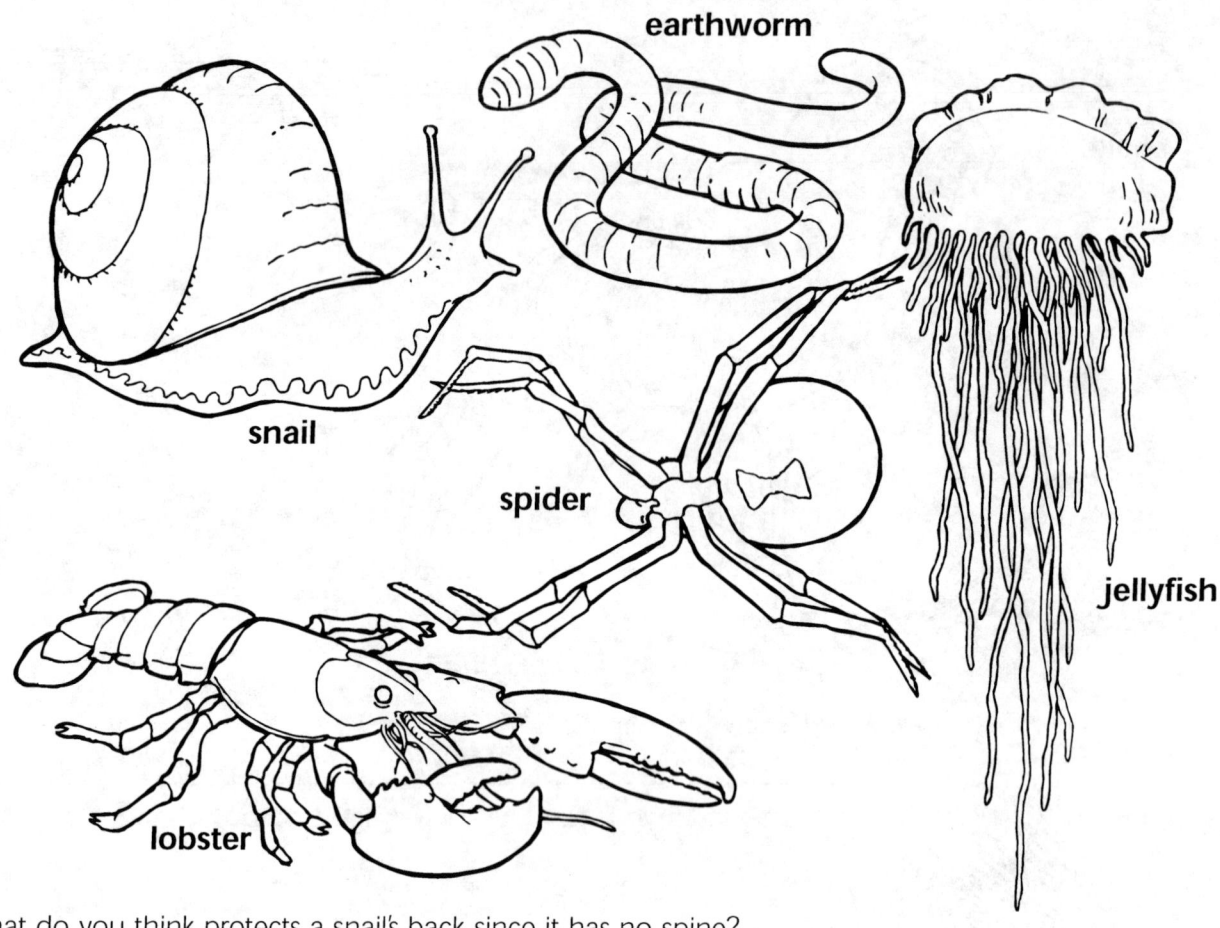

earthworm

snail

spider

jellyfish

lobster

What do you think protects a snail's back since it has no spine?

_____

Classify the creatures below as vertebrates (**v**) or invertebrates (**i**).

dog	_____	rabbit	_____	lion	_____
clam	_____	octopus	_____	earthworm	_____
mouse	_____	spider	_____	snail	_____
bird	_____	ant	_____	squirrel	_____
grasshopper	_____	butterfly	_____	chicken	_____
bat	_____	crab	_____	snake	_____
fish	_____	starfish	_____	deer	_____

Name _____   Date _____

Classification

CLASSES OF VERTEBRATES—MAMMALS

All animals belong to the Animal Kingdom. Kingdom is the largest classification group. Animals are then divided into **vertebrates** and **invertebrates**. Both vertebrate and invertebrate animals have several **classes**. There are five classes of vertebrate animals. Each has its own characteristics.

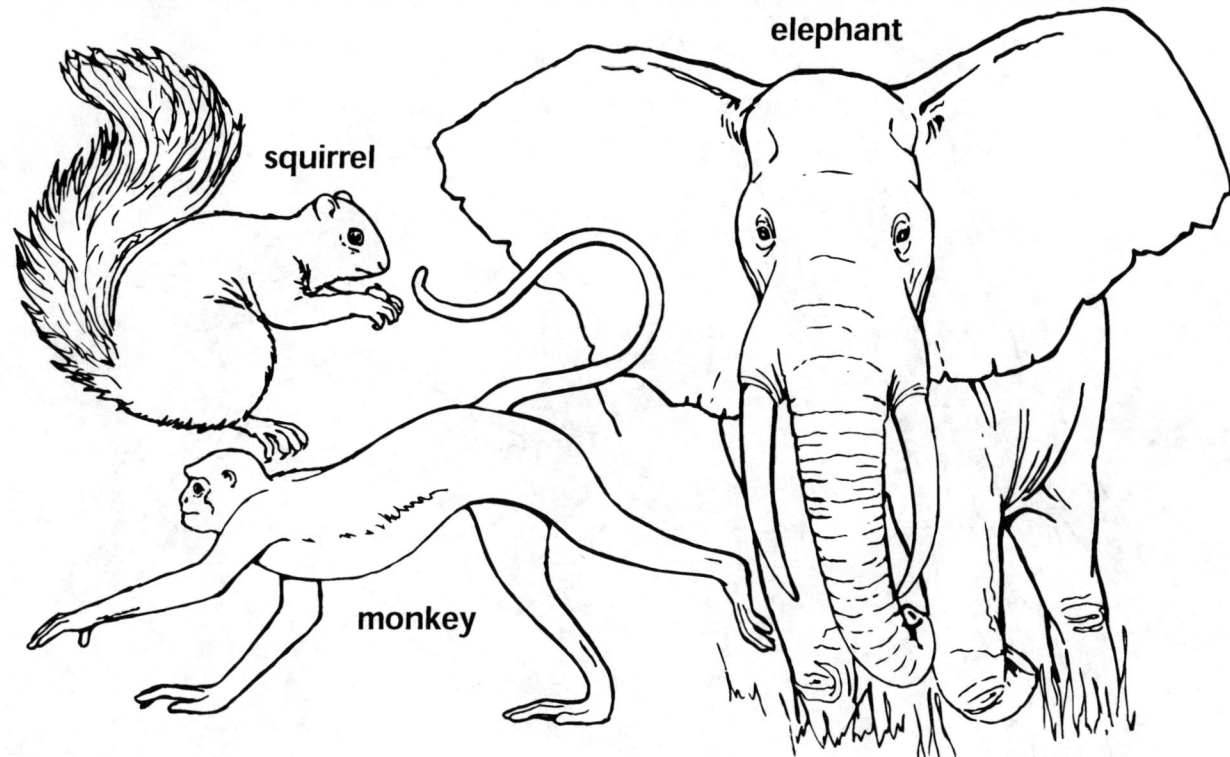

Characteristics of Mammals:
  1. They are warm-blooded;
  2. They give birth to live young;
  3. Their babies get milk from their mother's body;
  4. They have fur or hair on their bodies; and
  5. They have four limbs (whales and dolphins have flippers).

Name three other mammals. _____ _____ _____

1. Mammals come in all sizes and shapes and live almost everywhere. Look up and compare the largest animal that has ever lived—the blue whale—and the smallest mammal—a kind of shrew. How much does each weigh as an average adult, where does each live, and what else can you find out about them? Write your answers on another sheet of paper.

2. What mammal can fly? _____

3. What characteristic not mentioned above makes mammals such as dolphins, chimpanzees, and human beings different from other mammals? _____

MP3423 Classification   11   Copyright © 2000 – Milliken Publishing Co. All rights reserved.

Name _____ Date _____

CLASSIFICATION

CLASSES OF VERTEBRATES—BIRDS

parrot

cardinal

owl

Characteristics of Birds:
1. They are warm-blooded;
2. They hatch from eggs;
3. Feathers cover their bodies; and
4. They have two legs and two wings (very small wings make it impossible for some birds to fly).

Name three other birds. _____ _____ _____

1. Find out why a big bird such as the ostrich cannot fly. Name other birds that cannot fly and describe them. Write your answers on another sheet of paper.
2. Some of the bones in a bird's body are hollow. Use reference sources to find out how this affects flight. Write your answers on another sheet of paper.

Copyright © 2000 – Milliken Publishing Co. All rights reserved.

MP3423 Classification

Name _____   Date _____

CLASSIFICATION

CLASSES OF VERTEBRATES—REPTILES & AMPHIBIANS

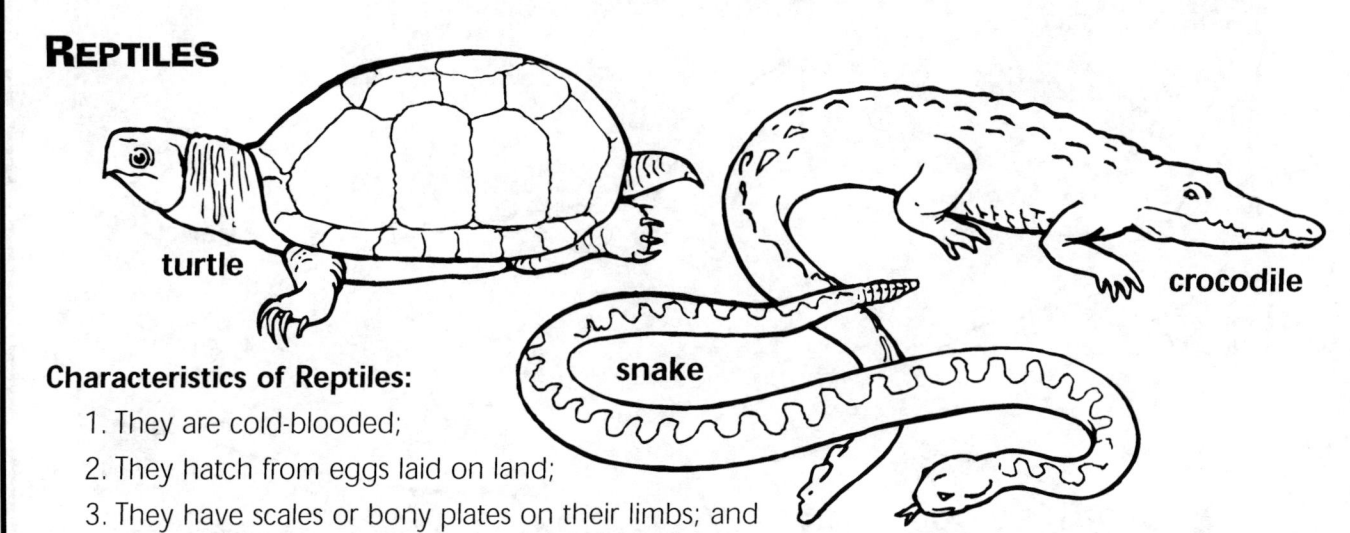

REPTILES

turtle

crocodile

snake

Characteristics of Reptiles:
  1. They are cold-blooded;
  2. They hatch from eggs laid on land;
  3. They have scales or bony plates on their limbs; and
  4. They have four short limbs or no limbs.

1. Dinosaurs were reptiles. They became extinct about 65 million years ago. Write a report about one type of dinosaur.

2. Describe how a snake sheds its skin.

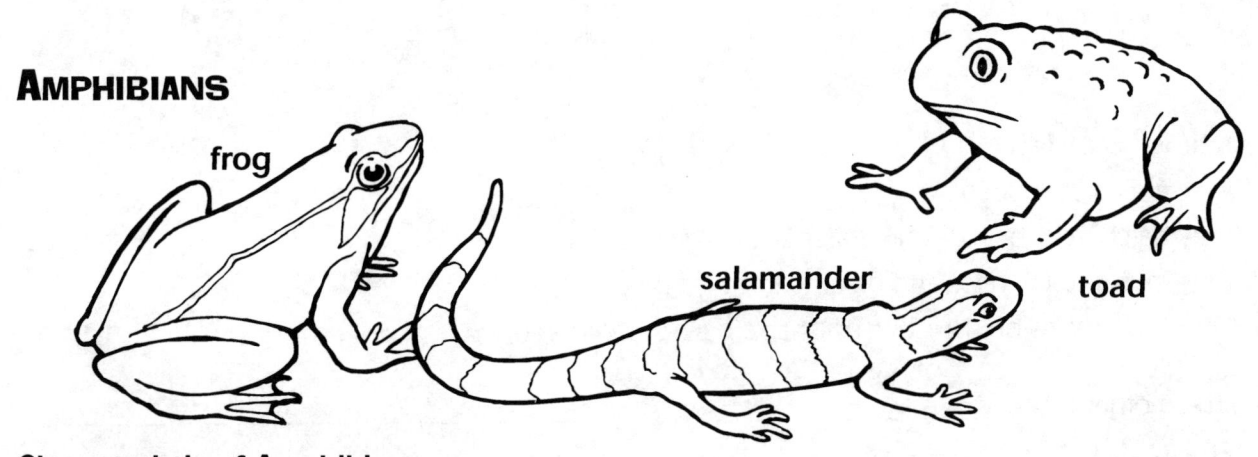

AMPHIBIANS

frog

salamander   toad

Characteristic of Amphibians:
  1. They are cold-blooded;
  2. They hatch from eggs laid in water or wet places;
  3. They have no scales, but smooth skin which must be kept wet;
  4. They use skin, as well as lungs, for breathing;
  5. They have four limbs; and
  6. Young animals breathe through their gills.

3. If *amphi* means "on both sides" or "around," and *bios* means "life," what does *amphibious* mean? Use a dictionary. How does this term apply to frogs?

MP3423 Classification   Copyright © 2000 – Milliken Publishing Co. All rights reserved.

Name _____   Date _____

CLASSIFICATION

CLASSES OF VERTEBRATES—FISH

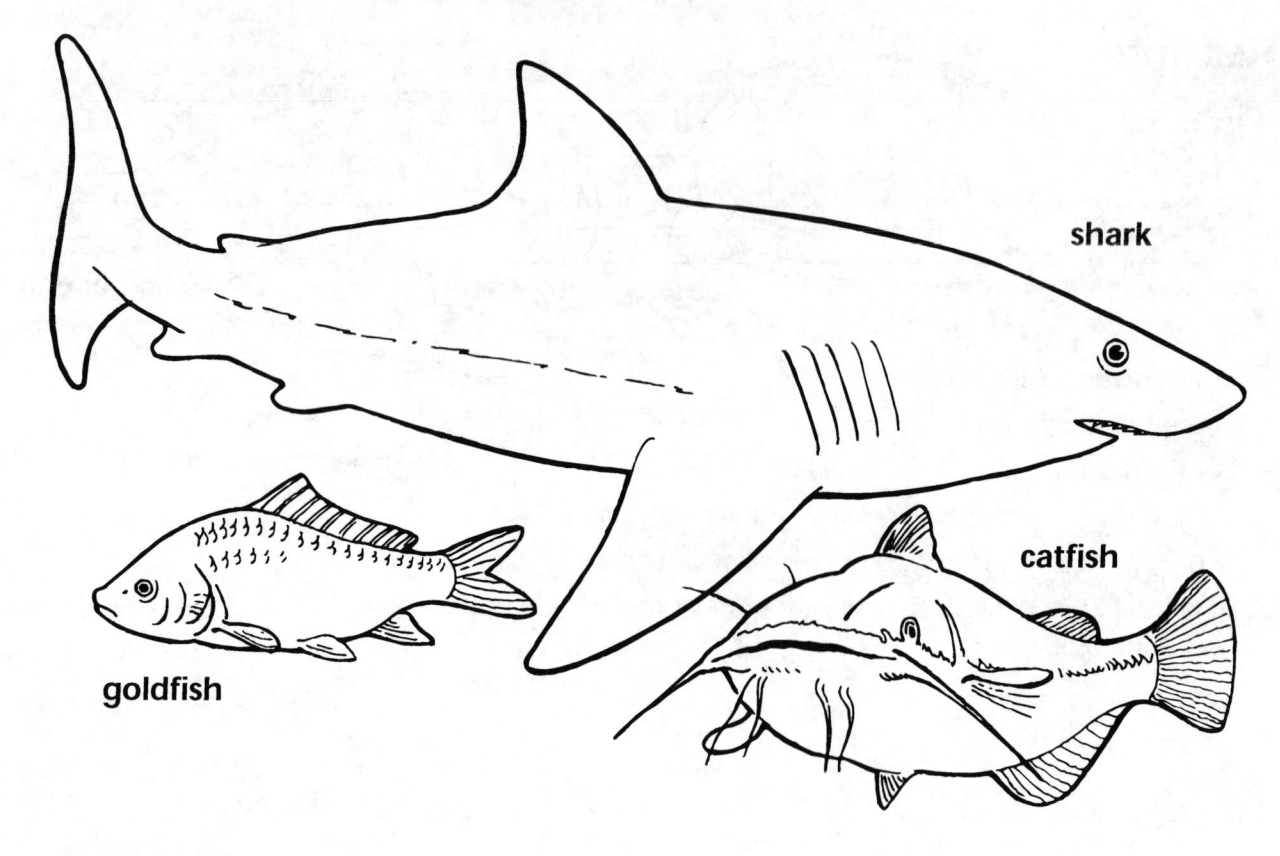

shark

goldfish

catfish

Characteristics of fish:
 1. They are cold-blooded;
 2. They hatch from eggs laid in water (sharks give live birth);
 3. They must live in water and breathe through their gills; and
 4. Most have scales on their bodies (sharks have smooth skin).

Name three other fish. _____ _____ _____

Write the class of vertebrate animal for each description.

1. It must keep its skin wet. _____
2. It breathes through gills. _____
3. It gets milk from its mother's body. _____
4. It has two legs and two wings. _____
5. It is hatched from an egg laid on land. _____

Name _____   Date _____

CLASSIFICATION

CLASSES OF INVERTEBRATES

There are many more invertebrates than vertebrates in the Animal Kingdom. There are also many more classes of invertebrates. Three of the larger classes of invertebrates are:

1. **Anthropods**—about 9,000,000 species
   Most live on land. Ants, bees and wasps have highly organized colonies. This class includes horseshoe crabs, spiders, and insects.

2. **Mollusks**—about 130,000 species
   Some of the largest invertebrates are in this class. It includes the giant clam and giant squid. Among the most intelligent are squid and octopus. This class includes snails, clams, and oysters.

3. **Platyhelminthes** (Flatworms)—about 13,000 species
   These creatures live in all habitats—land, water, as well as on other animals.

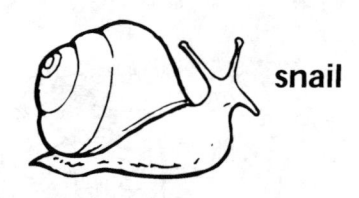

scorpion

snail

flatworm

Listed below are four kinds of bees, their habitats, and some of their characteristics. Fill in the letter for the most appropriate activity for each kind of bee.

    A. cuts ovals from leaves   C. produces honey

    B. attracted to perspiration   D. pollinates clove

	HABITAT	CHARACTERISTICS	ACTIVITY
Bumble bee	underground nest	longer mouth parts for better pollination	_____
Honey bee	hive	legs have "pollen baskets"	_____
Sweat bee	ground nest	small, brightly colored	_____
Leaf-cutting bee	underground nests lined with leaves	large, brightly colored	_____

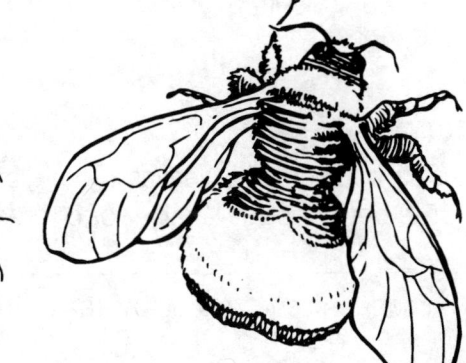

MP3423 Classification   15   Copyright © 2000 – Milliken Publishing Co. All rights reserved.

Name _____   Date _____

CLASSIFICATION

PLANT KINGDOM—VASCULAR

Another familiar biological kingdom is the Plant Kingdom. Plants are divided into two classes: vascular and nonvascular.

VASCULAR

Green plants can make food. Green plants have tubes to carry water and food through the plant. All green plants that have tubes are known as **vascular** plants.

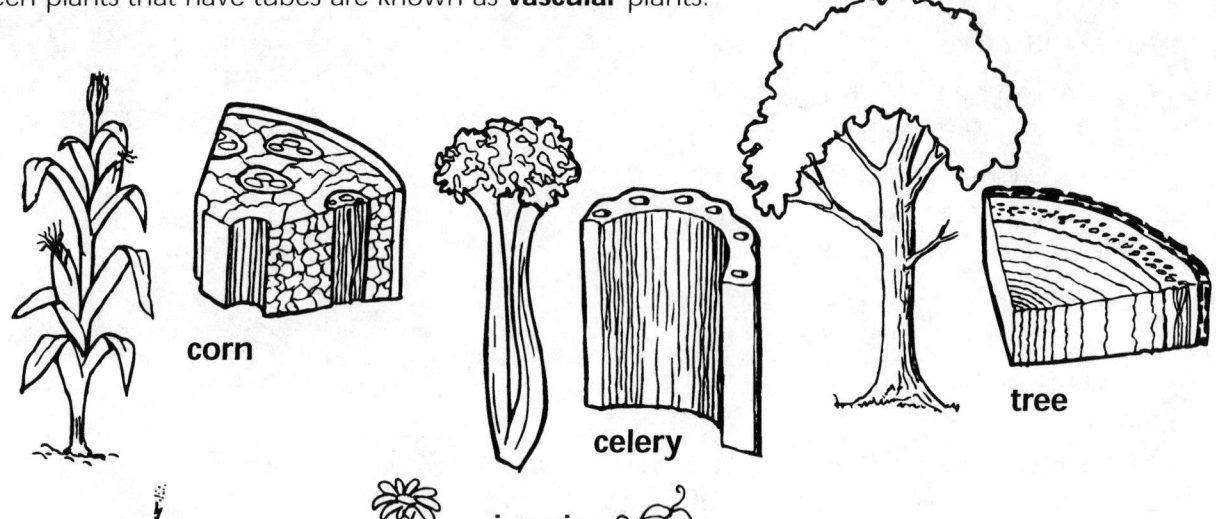

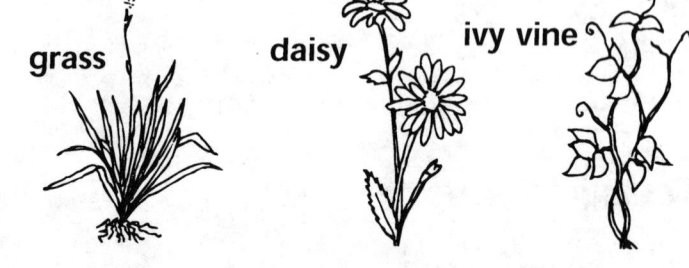

corn **celery** **tree**

grass **daisy** **ivy vine**

1. Green plants that have tubes, flowers, and fruits which produce seeds are called **angiosperms**.
2. Green plants with tubes, seed-making parts in cones, but no flowers are called **gymnosperms**.
3. Green plants with tubes, but no flowers, fruits or seeds are **ferns**. Ferns produce spores. Spores, like seeds, grow into new plants.

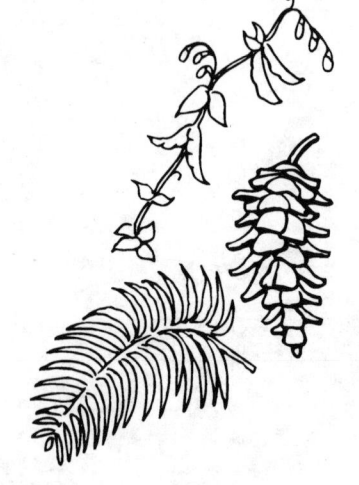

ACTIVITY

Place a stalk of celery with leaves into a glass of water colored with red food coloring. Cut a diagonal slice off the bottom edge. Wait two to three hours. What happens to the leaves?

_____

When a change occurs, cut across the stem to see the outline of the tubes.

Copyright © 2000 – Milliken Publishing Co. All rights reserved.   MP3423 Classification

Name _____ Date _____

CLASSIFICATION

PLANT KINGDOM—NONVASCULAR

Green plants that have no tubes are mosses and liverworts. They reproduce by spores, which are in tiny cases containing the seeds. As they fall to the earth, new plants germinate and sprout. Plants with no tubes are called nonvascular plants.

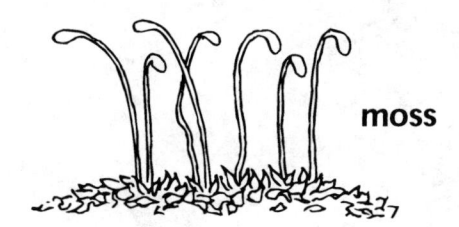

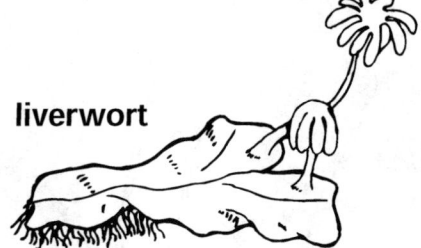

moss

liverwort

ACTIVITY

Dig moss and some surrounding soil from woods or yard. Gently transplant moss into a small terrarium. Water well and keep out of direct sunlight. When a stalk shoots up, look at its top with a magnifying glass. Find the capsule containing the spores. When the capsule opens, the spores will fall.

Write **A** for angiosperm,

Write **G** for gymnosperm.

Write **S** for plants which have spores.

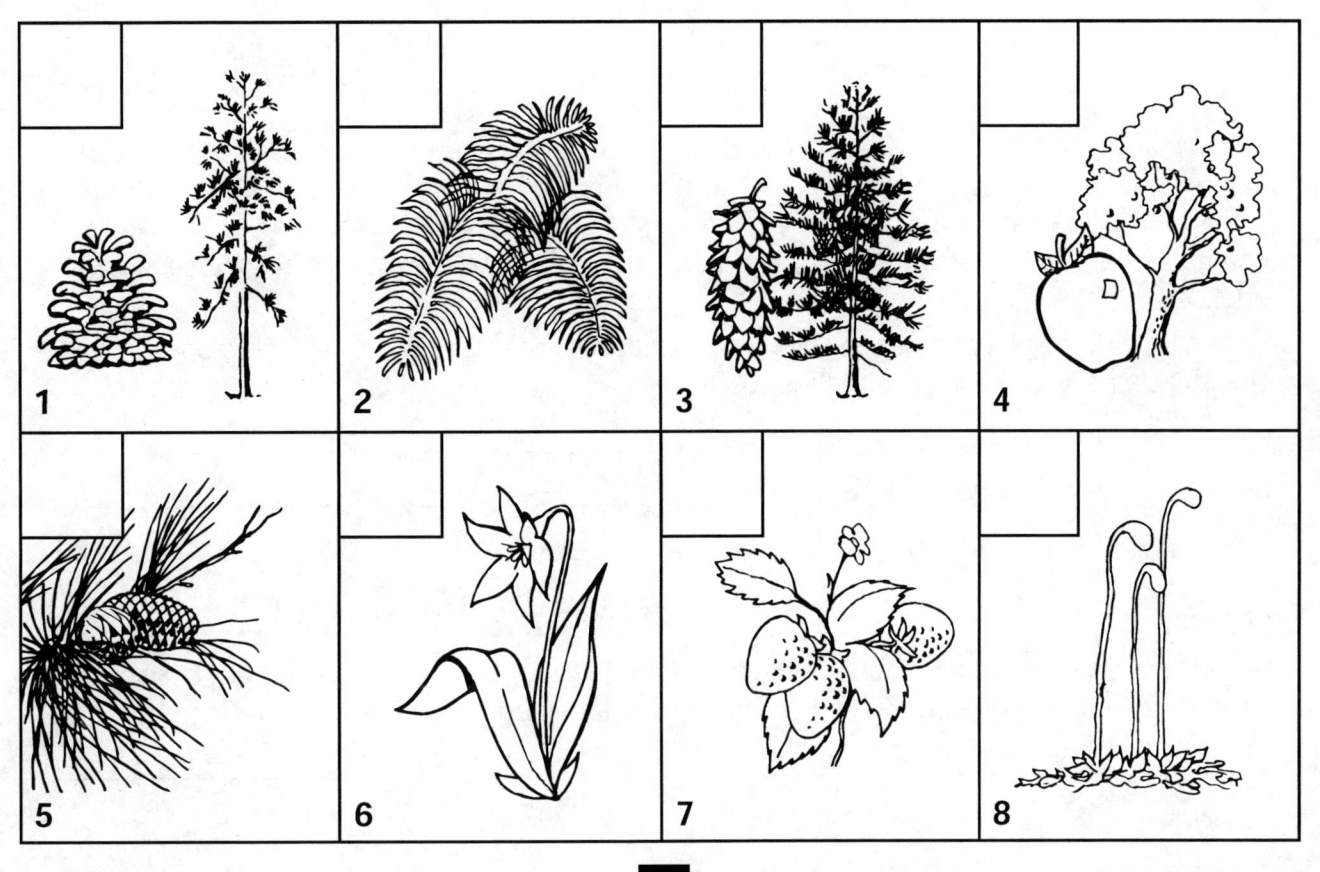

| 1 | 2 | 3 | 4 |
| 5 | 6 | 7 | 8 |

MP3423 Classification
Copyright © 2000 – Milliken Publishing Co. All rights reserved.

Name _____ Date _____

CLASSIFICATION

FUNGI KINGDOM

Until the discovery of the microscope, scientists classified all living things into animals and plants. With microscopes and other inventions, they were able to see many more differences in living organisms and added more kingdoms. One kingdom related to plants is called the **Fungi Kingdom**.

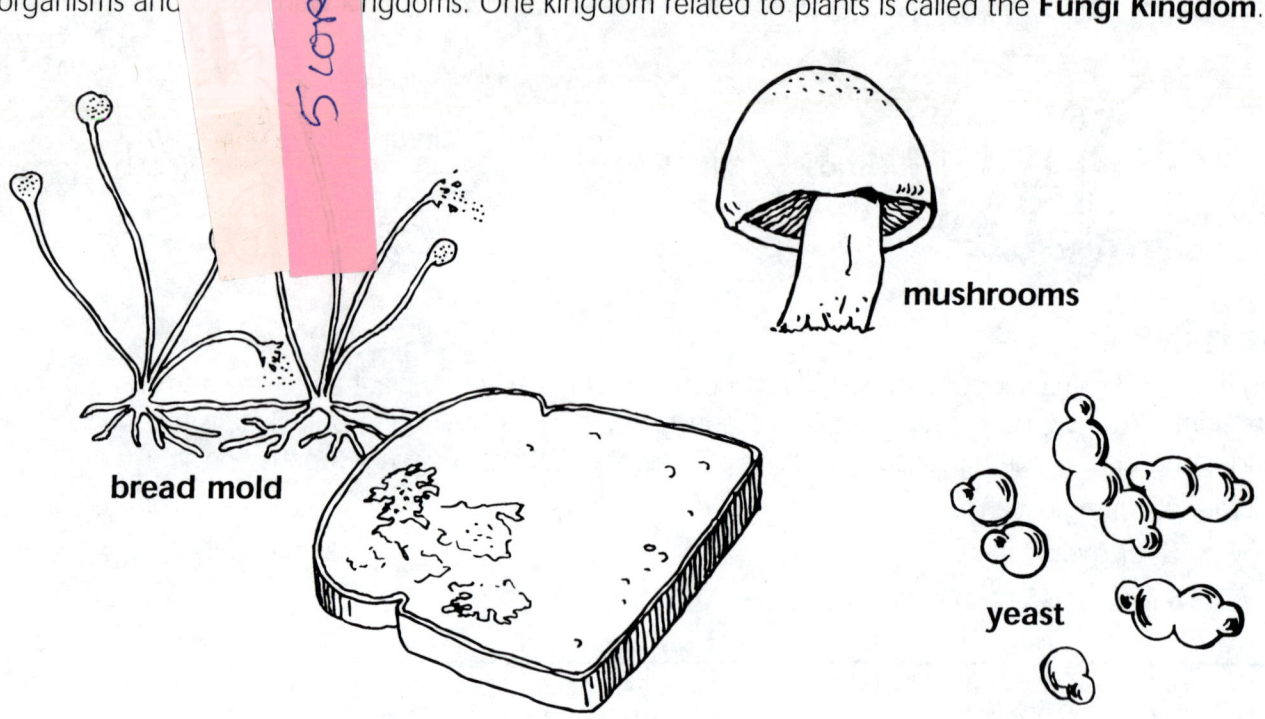

bread mold

mushrooms

yeast

Fungi are many-celled organisms which absorb food from living or dead organisms. Some grow in the soil. They give off juices that break down the cells of rotting plant and animal life. Fungi absorb the dissolved food. **Mushrooms** grow around rotting tree stumps. **Molds** grow on old, spoiled food and damp wood. **Mildew** grows on leather, wood, and cloth in damp places. All of these are forms of fungi.

Fungi can be both helpful and harmful. Some fungi attack food plants and spoil food crops. Others provide antibiotics like penicillin to fight infections.

1. What type of fungi grows on spoiled food? _____
2. What type of fungi grows on damp leather? _____
3. What type of fungi grows around rotting trees? _____

ACTIVITY

Place a slice of dry bread in a jar. Sprinkle the bread with water, cover with a lid and put in a warm, dark place. Observe the growth of mold on the bread. How long does it take to grow?

_____

Name _____   Date _____

CLASSIFICATION

PROTISTA KINGDOM

Scientists discovered other organisms that did not fit into the animal, plant, or fungi kingdoms. They created another kingdom of living things—the **Protista Kingdom**. It contains organisms that are complex, single cells.

Protozoans are a kind of protist found in pond water. Some feed on food like animals, while others make their own food. Some protozoans move around in search of food, while others live inside animals and feed on them. Some protozoans are parasites that cause disease in larger animals.

Blue-green and simple **algae** are also considered protists.

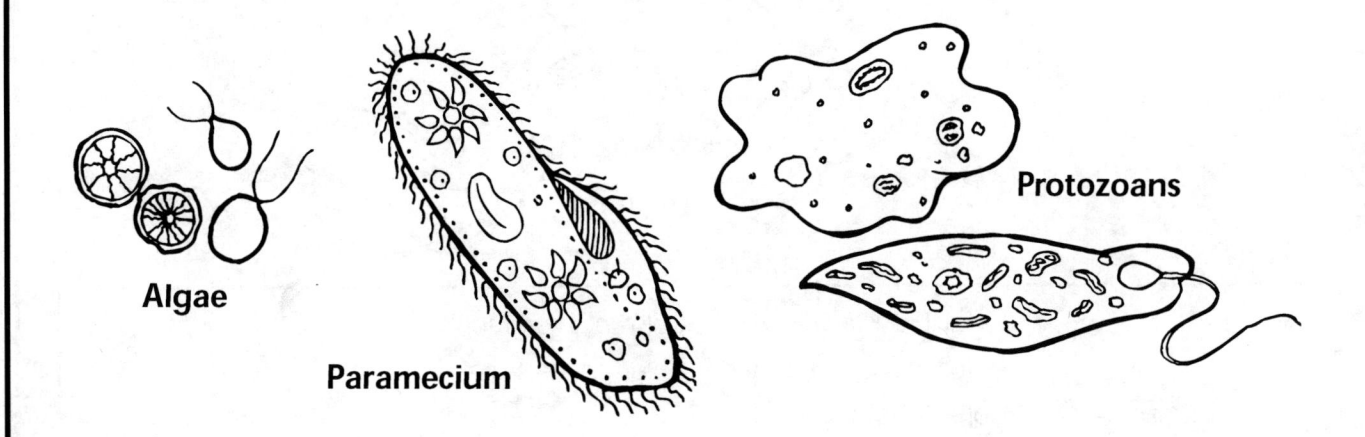

Algae

Paramecium

Protozoans

Look up the word parasite. Write a definition of it.
_____

Use a dictionary or other reference. Follow the path taken by the protist plasmodium to cause malaria in humans. Choose the right word and write it in the blank.

1. The plasmodium parasite lives in a _____.
   mosquito/housefly

2. It eventually reaches the salivary glands in the insect's _____.
   hand/mouth

3. The infected mosquito _____ a human.
   sits on/bites

4. The parasite is transferred to the _____ blood stream.
   mosquito's/human's

5. Finally the parasite reaches the human's liver from which it releases the infection that causes the disease _____.
   malaria/chicken pox

MP3423 Classification   19   Copyright © 2000 – Milliken Publishing Co. All rights reserved.

Name _____   Date _____

CLASSIFICATION

MONERA KINGDOM

The Monera Kingdom contains the smallest and most numerous of Earth's organisms. It includes **simple**, single cells. Some can make their own food; others cannot.

Bacteria are tiny living organisms, which are found everywhere living things exist. They are smaller than most other one-celled living things and are shaped like rods, spirals, and round balls. Some bacteria are used to produce cheeses. Some live in our intestines and help digest food. Harmful bacteria can cause disease.

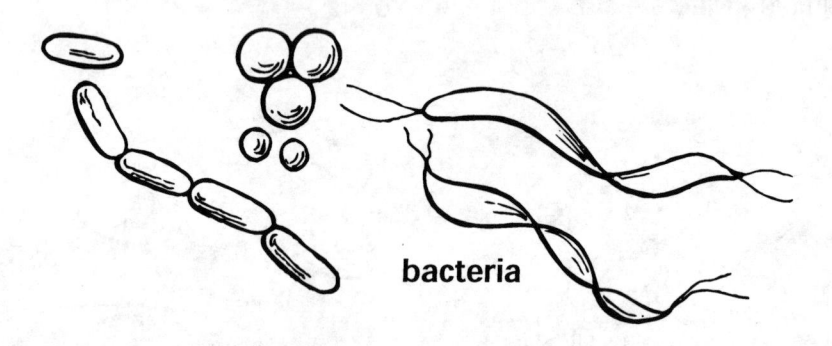

bacteria

Color protista yellow   Color plants green
Color monera orange   Color animals pink
Color fungi brown

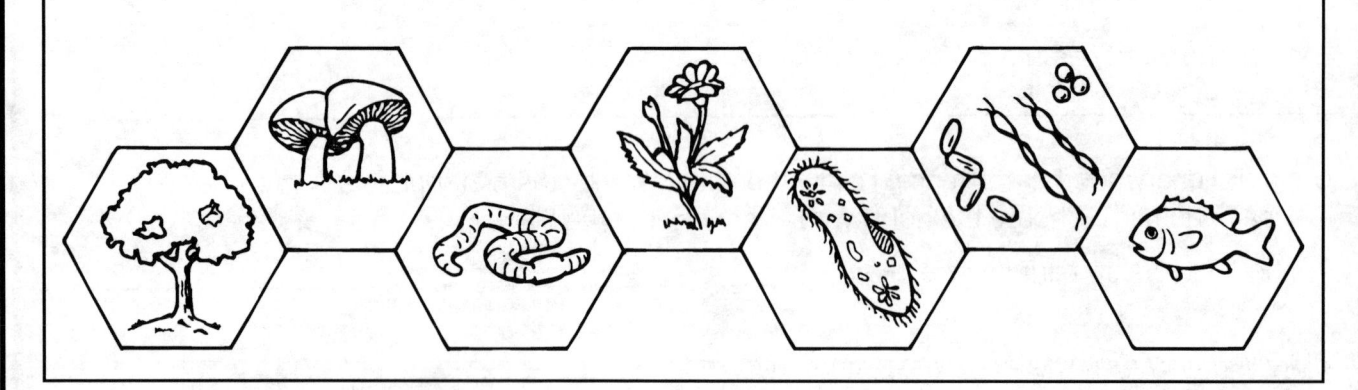

Write T for True or F for False.

1. _____ Monera is the name of a biological kingdom.
2. _____ Some bacteria are harmful.
3. _____ Bacteria are usually very large organisms.
4. _____ Bacteria cannot live in water.
5. _____ Bacteria can help us digest our food.

Copyright © 2000 – Milliken Publishing Co. All rights reserved.   MP3423 Classification

Name _____   Date _____

CLASSIFICATION

REVIEW

THE FIVE KINGDOMS OF LIVING ORGANISMS

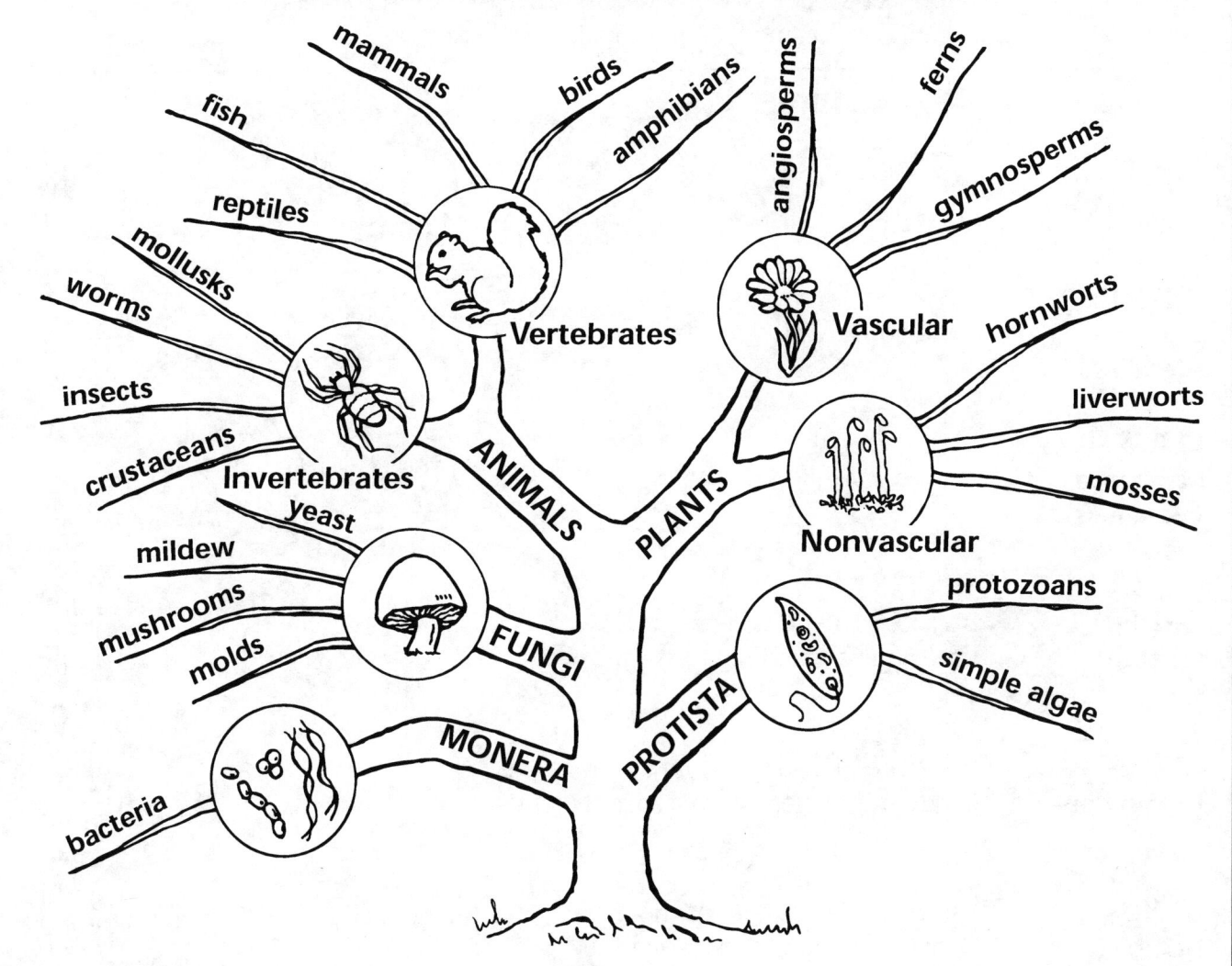

1. The smallest organisms are found in what kingdom? _____
2. All vertebrates have what in common? _____
3. The name for plants which have seed-bearing cones is _____.
4. Mushrooms are in what kingdom? _____
5. Name two plants without tubes. _____
6. Name five classes of vertebrates. _____
   _____
7. Name three classes of vascular plants. _____
   _____

MP3423 Classification   Copyright © 2000 – Milliken Publishing Co. All rights reserved.

Name _____   Date _____

CLASSIFICATION

CLASSIFICATION OF HUMANS

There are seven groups in the classification system of living organisms. As you go down the table below from kingdom to species, each group has more characteristics in common. Animals in a species have so many characteristics in common that they look much alike.

KINGDOM	CHARACTERISTICS	ANIMALS
ANIMALIA (Animals)		
PHYLUM Chordata (Vertebrates)	backbones	
CLASS Mammalia (Mammals)	backbones, nurse their young	
ORDER Primate	backbones, nurse their young, have fingers, stand nearly erect	
FAMILY Hominidae	backbones, nurse their young, have fingers, stand erect, have a special brain	
GENUS Homo	backbones, nurse their young, have fingers, stand erect, have larger brain, long life span	
SPECIES sapiens	backbones, nurse their young, have fingers, stand erect, even larger brain, long life span, high foreheads, thin skull bones	

Scientific name for humans—Homo sapiens (wise man)

1. At what point in the classification table above do the ape and man differ? _____
_____

2. Name three characteristics of the human that are different from the elephant. _____
_____

22

Copyright © 2000 – Milliken Publishing Co. All rights reserved.   MP3423 Classification

Name _____   Date _____

CLASSIFICATION

TAXONOMY

Taxonomy is the term for the science of plant and animal classification. It names all living things and puts them into groups to show relationships between them. Each living thing must have a name that is recognized all over the world. A scientific name is made up of two parts. The first part is called the **genus** and is written with a capital letter. The second name is the **species** and is not capitalized.

Scientific names are given in encyclopedias and dictionaries. It is important to use these scientific names as well as common names of living things when you write reports.

The genus name means that there are groups of living things that are very similar, but may be different in one or two important ways. A genus can contain two or more species. A species is a group that shares the same large structures.

The scientific name for dog is: **Canis familiaris.** The scientific name for cat is: **Felis domesticus.**

Use reference sources to find the scientific names of these organisms.

	genus	species
1. housefly	_____	_____
2. pineapple	_____	_____
3. lion	_____	_____
4. pussy willow	_____	_____
5. grizzly bear	_____	_____

Write the common name for each organism. Use a reference source if you need help.

genus

6. Rosa _____
7. Viola _____
8. Tulipa _____

species

9. leo _____
10. tigris _____
11. catus _____

Name _____   Date _____

CLASSIFICATION

LATIN, THE LANGUAGE OF CLASSIFICATION

Latin was the language used by ancient Romans. It is now considered a dead language, which means that it has not been the spoken language of any country for hundreds of years. Until modern times, scholars and scientists used written Latin in books and in letters read by educated people. Linnaeus used written Latin for his classification system. Today, scientists use New Latin, a language based on Latin and Greek.

Why do scientists use a dead language? They must name each plant and animal accurately by its scientific name. A spoken language, like English, changes as people create new words and give more meanings to old words. New Latin does not change. Scientists, who live in other parts of the world and speak many different languages, all read and understand New Latin. **Canis familiaris** is recognized as the scientific name for dog everywhere in the world! What do you think **familiaris** means?

Use the translated Latin words on the left, to give scientific names to the imaginary animals on the right.

Latin	English
sapiens	intelligent
elephans	elephant
canens	singing
mollis	weak
rana	frog
tres	three
felis	cat
canis	dog
auris	ear

1. A singing dog
   _____ _____

2. A three-eared cat
   _____ _____ — _____

3. A weak elephant
   _____ _____

4. An intelligent frog
   _____ _____

Copyright © 2000 – Milliken Publishing Co. All rights reserved.

MP3423 Classification

Name _____   Date _____

CLASSIFICATION

EXTINCT SPECIES

From a continuous study of the fossil remains of living things, scientists have learned that most of the species living on Earth in prehistoric times are **extinct** today. Extinct species of living things are placed in the classification system by their characteristics. In 1938, the Coelacanth, a fish thought to be extinct, was found off the coast of Africa. Scientists were able to identify it by comparing it to its fossil remains in museums. It is one of the few species of lung fish alive today.

Scientists know about dinosaurs from the fossils of their bones, footprints, and eggs found in very old rocks. Dinosaurs are classified as reptiles because many had bony plates on their bodies, four limbs, laid their eggs on land, and spent some time in or near water. Reptiles are usually classified as cold-blooded, but a species of dinosaurs thought to be warm-blooded has also been discovered.

The passenger pigeon, hairy mammoth (prehistoric elephant), and tyrannosaurus rex are examples of extinct animals.

Research and name other extinct animals.

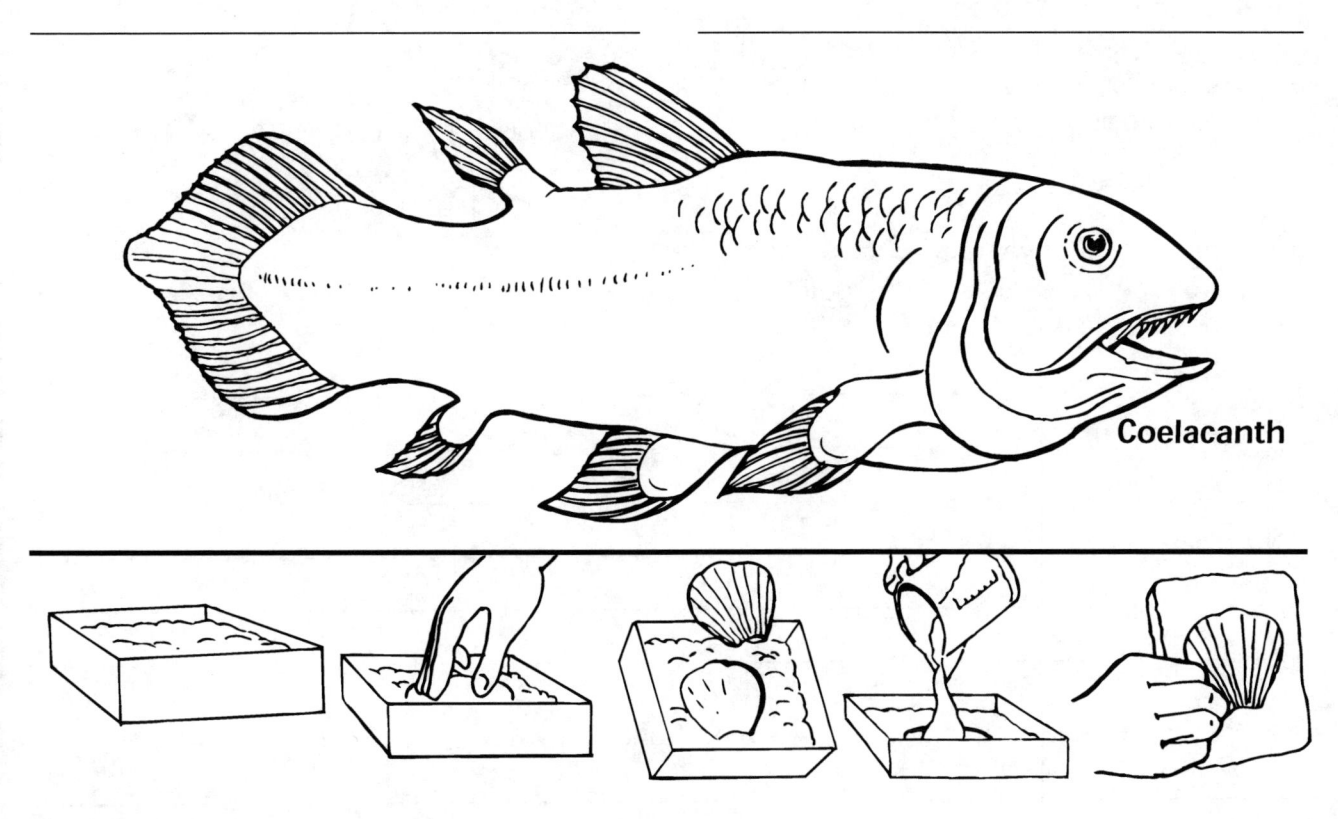

_____   _____

_____   _____

Coelacanth

ACTIVITY

Make your own fossil. Smooth a layer of modeling clay into a sturdy box top or plastic lid. Press bits of leaves, shells, or bone into the clay. Remove after the impression is made. Pour a plaster of Paris over clay and let harden. Remove the box and clay from the plaster to see your fossil.

Name _____ Date _____

CLASSIFICATION

ENDANGERED SPECIES

Today hundreds of plants and animals are in danger **(endangered)** of becoming extinct; that is, no longer living as a species. People continue to change the wilderness into cities. This often leaves plants and animals homeless. People pollute the air and water and this kills thousands of living things before they can reproduce more of their own kind. Too many species are being killed for sport and profit. Plants are taken from the desert and forest to be sold as houseplants to people in the cities.

We can protect these living things by enforcing laws which make it a crime to pollute the environment. We can set up animal refuges, bird sanctuaries, and plant preserves to protect the species we have. People of all ages must care enough about our wildlife to help protect it from extinction.

elephant

bison

tiger

There are many things you can do to help endangered species. Complete the suggestions below and add more of your own.

1. Talk to _____
2. Distribute information _____
3. Help _____
4. Stop _____
_____
_____

List 4 steps you would need to take to create a bird sanctuary.
_____
_____
_____
_____

Copyright © 2000 – Milliken Publishing Co. All rights reserved.

MP3423 Classification

The Classification System Today

Today scientists know that plants and animals change over long periods of time. Scientists look at large numbers of each species. They observe the differences (variations) among members of a species and try to discover what kind of common ancestor is the basis for the present species.

The study of fossil remains of earlier species helps in these discoveries. Also, scientists study **vestiges** in living members of a species. A vestige is a part of the body that is no longer needed, such as our appendix. The vestiges help scientists to understand that new plants and animals evolve or come from earlier forms in a species.

In 1900 a short-necked giraffe, the Okapi, was discovered. In 1938 the first living Coelacanth was found. In 1979 an unusual new species of shark was caught near Hawaii. It has huge lips, tiny teeth, and jaws four feet wide. It has been nicknamed "Megamouth." This new species as well as others constantly evolving from earlier ones are fitted into the classification system. Classification must always be open to growth and change.

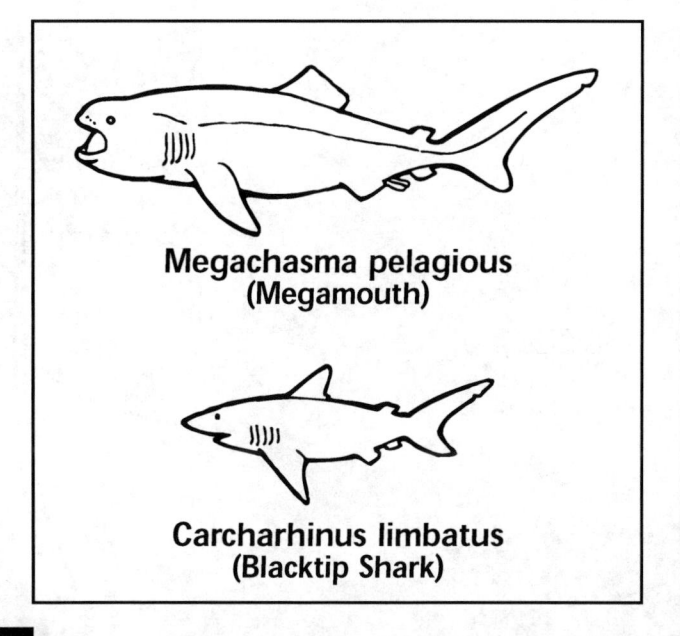

Below is a drawing of "Megamouth" and a shark from another species. Compare the two. Place an X in the correct box.

	Same	Similar	Different
1. size			
2. shape			
3. habitat			
4. mouth			
5. tail			
6. head			
7. top fin			
8. gills			

Megachasma pelagious (Megamouth)

Carcharhinus limbatus (Blacktip Shark)

Name _____   Date _____

CLASSIFICATION

REVIEW

Choose the correct word from the leaf below and write it in the blank space by its definition.

1. The invention that helped scientists discover new classification kingdoms _____
2. The name of the science of classification today _____
3. The language of classification _____
4. A species in danger of dying out is said to be _____
5. A place where animals cannot be hunted _____
6. It means a species is no longer living _____
7. The remains of plants and animals that died millions of years ago _____
8. The largest group in the classification system _____
9. The man who created the system of classification for plants and animals _____
10. The smallest group in the classification system _____

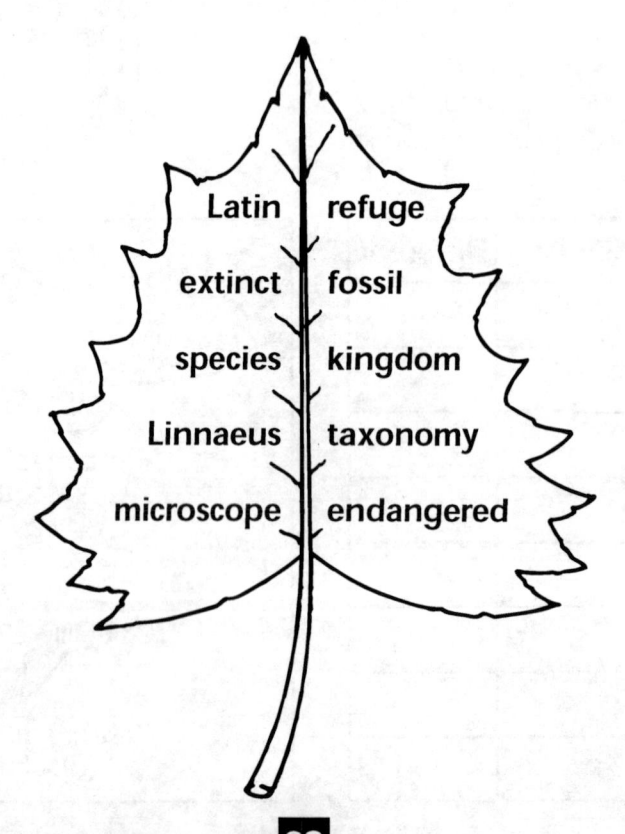

Word bank (on leaf):
Latin, refuge, extinct, fossil, species, kingdom, Linnaeus, taxonomy, microscope, endangered

Copyright © 2000 – Milliken Publishing Co. All rights reserved.

MP3423 Classification

CLASSIFICATION

BACKGROUND MATERIAL AND ACTIVITIES

Page 1: Classification is grouping by common attributes. Students are asked to group things that are alike in some way. The teacher may first ask for verbal responses. Point out, if not discovered, that a truck, airplane, and sailboat are used for transportation. The log, can of corn, and spool have a cylindrical shape, are round on both ends, and are grouped by shape. The bananas, oranges, and strawberries are food—all fruit. The swan and penguin are birds and living things. They have feathers, two feet, and wings. The pennant, pile of oranges, sail, and strawberries have triangular shapes. Draw out the generalization that there is more than one way to classify things.

Page 2: While this book is a study of biological (living) classification, make the student aware of the physical (nonliving) states: liquids, solids, and gases. Give examples of each. Minerals are one category of matter that have a classification system.

A classification scavenger hunt gives students experience in studying relationships between members of a group. Divide the class into five groups. Give each group a slip of paper with objects to be found in the classroom—metal, soft, bendable, round, multicolored, etc. As each group's collection is displayed, let others guess the category. This may also be used as an outdoor activity.

Page 3: Interest in classification began long ago. The zoo animals of a Chinese emperor were recorded as early as 1150 B.C. Later, kings exchanged exotic animals for amusement. In the 16th century, Pliny the Elder wrote books on zoology and medicinal botany. Gesner of Zurich wrote a detailed book on animals and is known as the "Father of Zoology." In 1735 Linnaeus created his system based on the similarities of anatomical structures. When he died, Chevalier de Lamarck carried on the work by classifying invertebrates.

Page 6: Make a skeleton for class study. Boil a chicken for 2 hours, remove meat and wash bones. Boil again in detergent and water until bones are bare and clean. Let dry in slow oven (200˚). Students can observe and arrange bones using a picture of a skeleton as a guide.

Page 7: Classification of biological organisms at bottom of page can be discussed. The tree and vine are green plants that take water from the soil. They make their own food in their leaves. They grow taller and thicker with age and have stomates—tiny openings on the underside of their leaves—which allow air to move into the plants. They react to seasonal changes by dropping leaves or forming grapes. The snake and horse must take in food, breathe oxygen, grow and reproduce. The snake lays eggs and the horse gives live birth. Mushrooms take food from the soil and grow by sending up fruiting bodies with gills underneath. In the gills are spores, which in the mature plant are carried off by the wind to reproduce in the ground. Plants take in air and give off gases. They do not breathe as people and animals do. Scientists use the word "respire" for the exchange of gases in plants.

Page 9: Make a model of a backbone (spinal column). String spools of the same size on a cord. Tie each end and show how the column can be bent and twisted. Ask students what the spool represents (vertebra) and what the cord would be (spinal cord). Cut disks about the same diameter as the spools from a sponge. Put a hole in the middle and string them on the cord between spools. Show how these "discs" protect vertebrae as the spine bends and twists.

Pages 16–17: Encourage students to bring pine cones for observation of differences. Shake cones to release the paper-thin seeds from between cone projections. Lead students to see similarities of cone-bearing plants: needle-like leaves, "evergreen" and triangular shape of tree crowns. Students may make a classroom collection of seeds to open, plant, or do art projects. Reinforce—seeds allow the plants to reproduce. Show a fern and the brown spore cases on underside of leaf. Show green moss, which has no true leaves, stems, or roots, but has stalks holding spore cases.

Pages 18–20: Fungi never form true roots, stems, or leaves. They do not have chlorophyll and must depend on the remains of dead organisms for food. Fungi keep the soil fertile. Note: Fungus uses the Latin plural form: Fungi.

Protozoans are one-celled organisms that can be seen under a microscope. Some live in ponds and salt water where they are eaten by small animals. Others cannot move and live inside an animal. They absorb food from the animal and are "parasites."

The algae which we know as seaweed are composed of millions of cells. They are classified as plants. Only simple, one-celled algae are classified as protists. Bacteria are needed to breakdown dead plants and animals, so that their former substances can be used again. These substances mix with soil and are drawn up with water by roots of plants. Bacteria are hard to kill. Their activity is slowed by freezing. Some viruses are also considered protists.

Page 21: Most—but not all—modern biologists and science texts accept the five kingdom classification. Explain that correctness of placement depends on the classification one is using. Use this situation to reinforce the idea that science is an open-ended field, constantly changing as better options are available.

Page 22: The teacher may wish to add classification of house cat for students' comparisons. Kingdom, Animalia; Phylum, Chordata; Class, Mammalia; Order, Carnivora (meat-eaters); Family, Felidae (lions, tigers, etc.); Genus, Felis (small cat); Species, domesticus (domesticated animal).

Page 24: From the Roman language, Latin, the languages of France, Italy, and Spain developed. Through the French language, words were introduced into the English or Anglo-Saxon language. When a new species is discovered, the person who made the discovery is given the honor of naming it—a possible incentive for inquiring students.

Page 25: Georgius Agricola coined the term "fossil" from "fodere"—"to dig" in Latin when miners dug up strange forms which did not fit into the system. The new sciences of geology and paleontology supported the concept of fossils as living things from the past.

Page 27: The Comte de Buffon, born the same year as Linnaeus, was the forerunner of the evolutionists. He looked for reasons for the changes in plants and animals over a long period of time. With such earlier thinking to lead the way, Darwin, about 100 years later developed his groundbreaking theory of natural selection. Discuss with students the possibility of the two sharks having a common ancestor.

CLASSIFICATION

ANSWERS

Page 1
Answers drawn from teacher presentation and background material.

Page 2
Accept appropriate answers.

Page 3
Answers will depend on leaves gathered.

Page 5
Ex.—round, hard
Ex.—fins, gills
Group: cow sheep deer
Group: turkey robin ostrich
Group: lizard crocodile
Group: rose tulip daisy

Page 6
1. whale
2. human
3. bat
4. dog
5. whale

Page 7
1. XXXXX
2. OOOOO
3. XXXXX
4. OOOOO
5. XXXXX
6. OOOOO
7. OXXXX
8. OOOOO
9. OOOOO
10. tree, snake, horse, mushroom, grapevine

Page 8

Across	Down
1. physical	2. structure
4. grows	3. air
6. group	5. solid
7. biology	
8. liquid	

Page 9
The backbone supports the body and shapes it. Bones help protect vital organs and help animals to move.

Page 10
The snail's shell

Vertebrates	Invertebrates
dog	clam
mouse	grasshopper
bird	octopus
bat	spider
fish	ant
rabbit	butterfly
lion	crab
squirrel	starfish
chicken	earthworm
snake	snail
deer	

Page 11
1. Blue whale: 100 feet long, weighs 100 tons. Shrew: less than 3 inches, weighs $1/14$ ounce.
2. Bats
3. They have a larger and more well developed brain

Page 12
1. The ostrich, emu, penguin, and kiwi cannot fly. Their ancestors could fly, but today these birds wings are too small to support the weight of their bodies in flight.
2. Hollow bones make flight easier because the bird's body is lighter.

Page 13
Amphibious means able to live in water or on land (live in two ways). Frogs begin life in water and then are able to live on land.

Page 14
1. amphibian
2. fish
3. mammal
4. bird
5. reptile

Page 15
D
C
B
A

CLASSIFICATION

Page 17
1. G
2. S
3. G
4. A
5. G
6. A
7. A
8. S

Page 18
1. mold
2. mildew
3. mushroom

Page 19
1. mosquito
2. mouth
3. bites
4. human's
5. malaria

Page 20
1. True — mushroom—brown
2. True — tree, plant—green
3. False — snake, fish—pink
4. False — protozoan—yellow
5. True — bacteria—orange

Page 21
1. monera
2. backbone
3. gymnosperm
4. fungi
5. moss, liverwort
6. mammal, bird, fish, reptile, amphibian
7. angiosperms, ferns, gymnosperms

Page 22
Family
Hominidae
no tail, fingers, large brain, stand erect

Page 23
1. housefly—Musca domestica
2. pineapple—Ananas comosus
3. lion—Panthera leo
4. pussy willow—Galix discolor
5. grizzly bear—Ursus horribilis
6. rose
7. violet
8. tulip
9. lion
10. tiger
11. cat

Page 24
1. Canis canens
2. Felis tres avlis
3. Elephans mollis
4. Rana sapiens

Pages 25–26
Accept appropriate answers.

Page 27
1. Different
2. Similar
3. Same
4. Different
5. Similar
6. Different
7. Different
8. Same

Page 28
1. microscope
2. taxonomy
3. Latin
4. endangered
5. refuge
6. extinct
7. fossils
8. kingdom
9. Linnaeus
10. species